Bedtime Collection

20 Favorite Bible Stories
and Prayers

ZONDERKIDZ

The Beginner's Bible® Bedtime Collection
Copyright © 2018 Zondervan
Illustrations © 2005, 2016 Zondervan

Requests for information should be addressed to:

Zonderkidz, 3900 Sparks Dr. SE, Grand Rapids, Michigan 49546

ISBN 978-0-310-76328-4

Scripture quotations marked NIrV are taken from the Holy Bible, *New International Reader's Version*®, NIrV®. Copyright © 1995, 1996, 1998, 2014 by Biblica, Inc.® Used by permission of Zondervan. All rights reserved worldwide. www.zondervan.com. The "NIrV" and "New International Reader's Version" are trademarks registered in the United States Patent and Trademark Office by Biblica, Inc.®

Zonderkidz is a trademark of Zondervan.

Printed in China

18 19 20 21 22 23 24 25 / DSC / 15 14 13 12 11 10 9 8 7 6 5 4 3 2 1

Contents

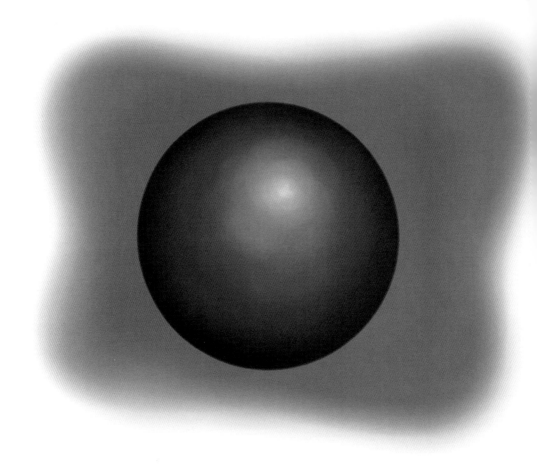

The Beginning

Genesis 1

In the beginning, the world was empty.
Darkness was everywhere.
But God had a plan.

God separated the light from the darkness.
"Let there be light!" he said.
And the light turned on.
He called the light "day."
And he called the darkness "night."
This was the end of the very first day.

Then God said, "I will divide the waters."
He separated the waters in the clouds
above from the waters in the ocean below.
He called the space between them "sky."
This was the end of the second day.

Next, God rolled back the waters
and some dry ground appeared.
He made plants of many shapes and colors.
He made mountains, hills, and valleys.
This was the end of the third day.

God put a shining sun in
the sky for daytime.
He put a glowing moon and twinkling
stars in the sky for nighttime.
This was the end of the fourth day.

On the fifth day,
God made swishy fish and
squiggly creatures to live in the ocean.
Then God made birds
to fly across the sky.

On the sixth day, God made animals
to creep, crawl, hop, and gallop.
Then from the dust, God made the most
wonderful creature of all—a person.
God named him Adam.
On the seventh day, God rested.

Goodnight Prayer

Thank you, God, for creating our beautiful world. Tonight, when I look at the stars, I will remember that you made them!

The heavens tell about the glory of God.
The skies show that his hands created them.
—Psalm 19:1

Adam and Eve

Genesis 2

God had planted a beautiful garden for
Adam in a place called Eden.
A river flowed through the garden.

Adam loved his new home.
His job was to name all the animals
and care for the garden.
Adam loved all the animals,
but he could not find a friend
that was just right for him.
So God created a woman.

Adam named her Eve.
She was just right for Adam.
Adam and Eve loved each other.
Together they took care
of God's garden.

Goodnight Prayer

God, thank you for giving me my family and friends. I am thankful that you made me part of your family too!

Honor your father and mother.
Then you will live a long time in the
land the LORD your God is giving you.
—Exodus 20:12

Noah's Ark

Genesis 6–9

After Adam and Eve left the garden,
many people were born.
The people kept doing bad things,
and they forgot about God.

Except Noah. Noah loved God.

God was sad that everyone but Noah
forgot about him.
He told Noah about his plan to start over.
"Make yourself an ark," God said.
"Here's how." So Noah and his family
began working on the ark.

When it was done, God said,
"Take your family and two of
every animal into the ark."
Animals creeped, crawled, hopped,
and galloped onto Noah's new boat.

After everyone was inside,
the rain began to fall.
And fall. And fall.
The ark rocked this way and
that way on the rising water.

Finally, the rain stopped.
Water covered everything!
Everyone inside the ark was safe.
Noah and his family were very happy.

The ark finally came to rest on
the top of a mountain.
God told Noah to leave the ark.
Noah and his family praised God.
God put a beautiful rainbow in the sky.
It was a sign of his promise to
never flood the whole earth again.

Goodnight Prayer

Thank you, God, for always keeping your promises. When I see a rainbow, I will remember how much you love me!

*Here is what God has promised us.
He has promised us eternal life.
—1 John 2:25*

Samson

Judges 13; 16

The Israelites were in trouble again.
Along came a very strong man
named Samson. God had chosen
him to save the Israelites from
their enemies, the Philistines.

Samson knew that as long as
he did not cut his hair,
he would always be very strong.

Samson was in love with Delilah.
The Philistines told Delilah they
would pay her if she found out
what made Samson so strong.
At first, Samson lied to her.

"If you tie me up with ropes,"
Samson said, "I will lose my strength."
That night while Samson slept,
Delilah tied him up. Then she shouted,
"The Philistines are coming!"
Samson jumped up and broke the ropes.
Delilah kissed him and asked,
"Won't you tell me your secret?"

Samson gave in and told her,
"My strength is in my long hair."
When Samson was asleep,
Delilah had all his hair cut off.
Samson's strength was gone!
The Philistines grabbed him
and put him in jail.

A while later, the Philistines were having
a big party. They brought Samson in
and made fun of him.
Samson prayed to God to make him
strong one last time. God did.
Samson pushed the pillars with all his might.
The temple came crashing down, and
Samson defeated the Philistines.

Goodnight Prayer

God, thank you for giving me strength in hard times. At night if I get scared, I will remember that you are with me!

God gives us strength. He is always there to help us in times of trouble.
—Psalm 46:1

David and Goliath

1 Samuel 17:1–51

The Philistines were enemies of God.
Their army came to fight King Saul's army.
A giant soldier named Goliath yelled, "Bring
out your best soldier to fight me!"

"If your strongest soldier defeats me,
we will be your slaves!" he boomed.
"If I defeat him, you will be our slaves!"
King Saul's soldiers were afraid.
They did not want to fight the giant.

Meanwhile, young David was taking
food to his brothers. They were
soldiers in King Saul's army.
When David reached the camp,
he saw Goliath. David heard the
giant's challenge.

"I am not afraid to fight the giant,"
said David. King Saul called for
David and told him, "You cannot fight
the giant. You are too young."
David replied, "God will be with me."

King Saul gave his armor to David,
but it was big and heavy.
David wasn't used to wearing armor.

David went to a nearby stream
and picked up five stones.
He stood before Goliath.
The giant laughed at him, but
David didn't care. He said,
"I come before you in the name
of the LORD who rules over all."

David put a stone in his sling
and ran toward the giant.
Then he let the stone fly.

It hit Goliath's forehead,
and he fell to the ground!
The Philistines saw that their hero
was dead. They ran away.

Goodnight Prayer

Thank you, God, for taking such good
care of me. Like a shepherd takes care
of his sheep, you always watch out for me!

The LORD is my shepherd.
He gives me everything I need.
—Psalm 23:1

(Read the rest of Psalm 23 with a parent.)

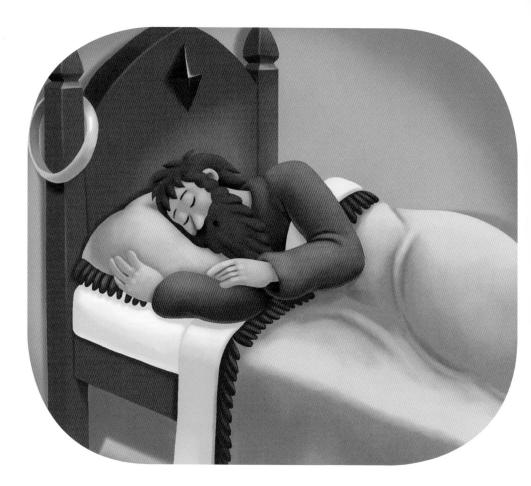

The Wise King

1 Kings 3:5–10:13

King Solomon loved God very much.
God spoke to him in a dream.
"Ask for anything you want," God said.

King Solomon answered,
"Give me wisdom so that I will know
the difference between right and wrong."
God was pleased with Solomon's answer.
"I will give wisdom to you," God said.
"I will also give you riches and honor."

King Solomon was wiser than any
other person. He spoke 3,000 proverbs,
or wise sayings, and wrote over 1,000
songs. He knew many things about
plants and animals.

King Solomon ordered thousands
of workers to build a temple for God.
When the temple was finished,
it was beautiful! King Solomon planned
a celebration.

All the people of Israel came
to see the temple. They were happy
to have a new place to worship.
They all said, "God is good.
His love lasts forever!"

Goodnight Prayer

∼

God, please make me wise like Solomon.
When I have to make a big choice,
I will always pray to you first.

*If any of you needs wisdom, you should
ask God for it. He will give it to you.*
—James 1:5

The Brave Queen

Esther 1–10

Esther was Jewish. That means she was
an Israelite. She lived in the land of Persia
with her older cousin Mordecai.

The king of Persia needed a new queen.
He announced, "Bring me the most
beautiful women from all over my
kingdom." Esther was one of the women
sent to the palace. When the king met
Esther, he chose her to be his queen.

Haman was the king's chief helper.
He hated the Jewish people. They were
God's people. Haman wanted everyone
to bow down to him. Mordecai refused
to bow down to Haman. Mordecai would
only bow down to God.

Haman went to the king. He said,
"The Jews are bad people. You should sign
a law that will help me get rid of them."
So the king signed the new law.
God's people were in great danger!

Mordecai heard about the new law.
He ran to tell Esther, "You must save
yourself and the rest of God's people.
Perhaps God has made you the
queen for this reason."
So Esther came up with a plan.
It would be very risky for her.

Esther invited the king and Haman to
a special dinner. Then she asked the king,
"Why does Haman want to get rid of me?"
The king was surprised. She said,
"I am Jewish. Haman tricked you into
signing a new law that would get rid of all the Jews."

The king told his guards, "Arrest Haman!"
Then he made Mordecai his new
chief helper. He told Queen Esther,
"I will make a new law that will keep
you and your people safe."
God used Esther to save his people!

Goodnight Prayer

God, please make me brave like Esther.
Give me courage when I feel afraid.

Be strong and brave. Do not be afraid.
*Do not lose hope. I am the L*ORD *your God.*
I will be with you everywhere you go.
—Joshua 1:9

Daniel and the Lions

Daniel 6

Darius became the new king of Babylon. Daniel was his chief helper. The king's other helpers did not like Daniel.

They said to the king, "You are such a wonderful king. You should make a new law that for the next 30 days, everyone must pray only to you. If they disobey, they will be thrown into the lions' den."

King Darius made the new law, but
Daniel kept praying to God because
Daniel loved God. The king's helpers
caught him praying.

They told King Darius, "Now you must
throw Daniel into the lions' den."
The king knew he had been tricked,
but he had to obey his new law.

Daniel was thrown into the lions' den.
He was not afraid. He knew God would
take care of him. King Darius told Daniel,
"I hope your God will save you."
That night, the king could not sleep.
He was too worried about Daniel.

At sunrise, the king hurried to the lions' den. "Has your God saved you from the lions?" he called. "Yes!" answered Daniel. "My God sent his angel to protect me." So Daniel returned to the palace. Then King Darius ordered everyone to honor and respect God.

Goodnight Prayer

God, give me a faith as big as Daniel's!
Help me to always trust in you.

Trust in the LORD with all your heart.
Do not depend on your own understanding.
In all your ways obey him. Then he will make
your paths smooth and straight.
—Proverbs 3:5–6

Jonah and the Big Fish

Jonah 1:1–3:10

Jonah was a prophet of God.
One day, God told Jonah,
"Go to the big city of Nineveh.
Tell them to stop doing bad things."

But Jonah ran away. He did not want
to go to Nineveh. Instead he got on
a boat to sail across the sea.
God sent a big storm to stop Jonah.
The sailors on the boat were afraid.
They thought the boat was going to sink!

Jonah told the sailors,
"My God has sent this storm.
If you throw me into the water,
the sea will become calm again."

So the sailors threw Jonah
into the raging sea.
Instantly, the sea became calm.

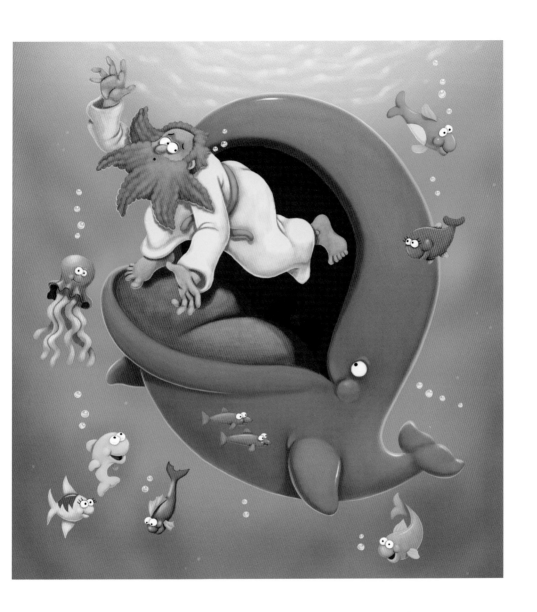

Just then, Jonah saw a big fish coming!
Gulp! The fish swallowed Jonah.

For three days and nights, Jonah was
inside the fish. He prayed to God,
"Please forgive me."

Then God told the fish to spit Jonah onto
dry land. God told Jonah a second time,
"Go and tell the people of Nineveh
to stop doing bad things."

This time, Jonah obeyed God.
The people in Nineveh
were sorry for doing bad things,
so God forgave them.

Goodnight Prayer

God, I know that sometimes I do the wrong thing. Thank you for forgiving me. Thank you for loving me even when I mess up.

If we confess our sins, he will forgive our sins. He will forgive every wrong thing we have done.
—1 John 1:9

Baby Jesus Is Born

Luke 2:1–7

Mary loved Joseph. Mary and Joseph
were going to be married soon.
Joseph lived in Nazareth, but his
family lived in Bethlehem.

A new leader named Caesar ordered all
people to go back to their homeland.
He wanted to count all the people
in his kingdom. So Mary and Joseph
went to Bethlehem.

Mary was going to have her baby soon.
When they arrived in Bethlehem,
they looked for a safe place to sleep,
but all the inns were full.

Finally, a man was able to help them.
He said, "I do not have any rooms left,
but you are welcome to sleep
in the stable."

Joseph made a warm place for Mary
to rest. While they were there,
little baby Jesus was born.

Mary wrapped Jesus in strips of cloth
and gently laid him in a manger.

Goodnight Prayer

God, thank you for sending your one and only son, Jesus. You kept him safe and warm, just like you keep me safe and warm as I go to sleep.

The Lord himself will give you a sign. The virgin is going to have a baby. She will give birth to a son. And he will be called Immanuel.
—Isaiah 7:14

Shepherds Visit

Luke 2:8–20

On the night Jesus was born,
shepherds were watching their sheep.
Suddenly, an angel stood before them,
and God's light shined all around.

The angel said, "Do not be afraid. I bring joyful news to all people. Today, in the town of Bethlehem, a Savior has been born! He is lying in a manger."

Then a choir of angels appeared.
They sang, "Glory to God in the highest!
Peace and goodwill to everyone on earth!"

The shepherds rushed to Bethlehem.
There they found baby Jesus.
They told Mary and Joseph
what the angel said.

As they returned to their sheep,
the shepherds told everyone what they
had seen and heard. All along the way,
the shepherds shouted praises to God.

Goodnight Prayer

Jesus, thank you for coming to be with us! Just like the shepherds long ago, I'm going to tell everyone about you and all the good things you have done for me.

After the shepherds had seen him, they told everyone. They reported what the angel had said about this child. All who heard it were amazed at what the shepherds said to them.
—Luke 2:17–18

Jesus Chooses His Disciples

Matthew 4:18–22; 9:9; 10:1–4; Mark 1–3; Luke 5–6

Jesus began to tell people about God.
He knew he had a lot of work to do,
and he went to find some helpers.

Jesus chose good people.
Their names were Peter, Andrew, James,
John, Philip, Bartholomew, Thomas, and
another man named James.

JOHN

JAMES
SON OF ZEBEDEE

PETER

MATTHEW

ANDREW

Matthew, Thaddaeus, Simon, and Judas
joined them too. Jesus now had twelve new
followers. He called them his disciples. Jesus
taught them about God's love.

Goodnight Prayer

Jesus, you made friends with all kinds
of people while you were here on earth.
I'm so glad you're my friend too!

"Come and follow me," Jesus said.
"I will send you out to fish for people."
—Mark 1:17

Jesus Teaches on a Mountain

Matthew 5:1–12; 6:25–34; Luke 6:17–23; 12:22–31

All sorts of people went to see Jesus.
Children, mothers, fathers,
grandmas, and grandpas.
They all wanted to hear what
he was teaching.

"Look at the birds," said Jesus.
"Do they store up food in a barn?
No. God feeds them."

"Look at the flowers," said Jesus.
"They don't work or make clothes.
God dresses them in lush leaves
and pretty petals."

Then Jesus said, "You are much more important than birds. You are much more important than flowers.
So do not worry. If God takes care of them, God will take care of you."

Goodnight Prayer

Sometimes I worry too much. Jesus, please help me not to worry. I know you will give me everything I need.

Put God's kingdom first. Do what he wants you to do. Then all those things will also be given to you.
—Matthew 6:33

The Lord's Prayer

Matthew 6:9–13; Luke 11:1–4 (NIV)

When Jesus was on the mountain,
he taught the people how to pray.
Jesus said,

"Our Father in heaven,
hallowed be your name,
your kingdom come,
your will be done
on earth as it is in heaven.
Give us today our daily bread.
Forgive us our debts,
as we also have forgiven our debtors.
And lead us not into temptation,
but deliver us from the evil one."

Amen.

Goodnight Prayer

Thank you, Jesus, for listening no matter where I am. Even when I'm alone, I always have a friend I can talk to.

At all times, pray by the power of the Spirit. Pray all kinds of prayers.
—Ephesians 6:18

Jesus Calms the Storm

Matthew 8:23–27

Jesus and his disciples got into a boat.
They wanted to cross the sea.

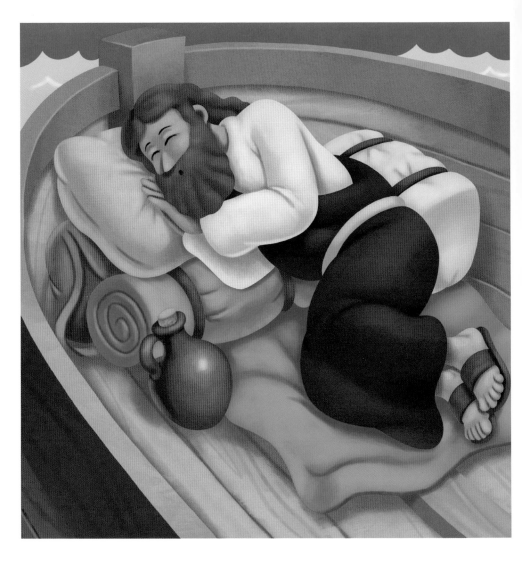

Jesus took a nap.
The waves gently rocked
the boat back and forth.

Suddenly a great storm came up.
Waves splashed over the boat.
Winds whipped around the disciples.

They woke Jesus up and shouted,
"The boat is sinking! Don't you care?"

Jesus asked, "Why are you so afraid?
Don't you have any faith at all?"
Then Jesus told the storm to stop.
Right away it was calm.

The disciples were amazed. They said
to each other, "Who is this man Jesus?
Even the wind and the waves obey him!"

Goodnight Prayer

Dear Jesus, there are times when
I'm afraid. But I can always trust you to
help me through life's scary storms.

In you, LORD my God, I put my trust.
—Psalm 25:1

The Lost Sheep

Matthew 18:10–14; Luke 15:3–7

Some people wondered who was
most important to God. So Jesus
told them a parable.

"Think about a shepherd. What does he do? He watches over his sheep. He gives them plenty of food, and he gives them plenty of water."

"He counts them up to make sure
they are all there. If one is lost,
he looks for it. He looks in the barn.
He looks near the stream. He looks
in the hills. He looks everywhere."

"The shepherd does not give up.
At last, he finds the little lost sheep!"

"He carries the sheep back.
He calls his friends together
and says, 'Let's celebrate!
My lost sheep has been found!'"

Then Jesus said, "God loves every one
of his children like a shepherd loves his
sheep. When one of them sins, it is like
a sheep that has gone astray, and God is
very sad. But when the person turns away
from sin and comes back to God, he is
very, very happy. He celebrates like a
shepherd who has found his lost sheep."

Goodnight Prayer

God, no matter what I do or where I go,
I know you always care about me. Thank you
for coming to find me when I'm lost!

*The L<small>ORD</small> will watch over your life no
matter where you go, both now and forever.*
—Psalm 121:8

The True King

Matthew 21:1–11; Mark 11:1–11; Luke 19:29–42; John 12:12–19

Jesus and his disciples went to Jerusalem
for the Passover Feast. Jesus told
two disciples to bring him a donkey.
He told them where to find it.

Jesus rode the donkey to Jerusalem.
A big crowd welcomed him.

People waved palm branches and put
them on the road in front of Jesus.

They shouted, "Hosanna! Hosanna!
Blessed is the king of Israel!"

The leaders in Jerusalem did not
like Jesus. They saw how many people
were following him, and they were
angry about it. They were jealous.

Goodnight Prayer

Jesus, you are the true King. You didn't have to come be with us, but you did because you love us! Thank you for coming.

Blessed is the king who comes
in the name of the Lord!
—Luke 19:38

Jesus Is Arrested
and Crucified

Matthew 26–27; Mark 14–15; Luke 22–23; John 18–19

Judas went to the leaders. He asked,
"How much will you pay me if I help
you capture Jesus?" They said,
"Thirty pieces of silver." So Judas took
the money and made a plan.

Jesus had gone to his favorite garden
to pray. The disciples went along.
Jesus prayed, "Father, if it is your will,
I am ready to give my life so that
all the people who trust in me will be
saved from their sins."

Soon, Judas arrived with some soldiers.
Peter wanted to protect Jesus.
But Jesus said, "No. I must allow this
to happen." All the disciples ran away,
and the soldiers arrested Jesus.

The soldiers took charge of Jesus.
They made him carry a big wooden cross.
They took him to a place called
The Skull (*Golgotha*).
There they nailed Jesus to the cross.

Jesus died on the cross. Everyone who loved Jesus was very sad. But they forgot something important. Jesus had said he would see them again soon!

Goodnight Prayer

Jesus, even though it was scary,
you still gave your life to save
the world. Thank you so much!

*God so loved the world that he gave his
one and only Son. Anyone who believes in
him will not die but will have eternal life.
—John 3:16*

Jesus Returns

John 20:19–20

The disciples had locked themselves in a small room because they were afraid the leaders would send soldiers to arrest them.

Suddenly, Jesus appeared to them!
He said, "Peace be with you."
They thought he was a ghost. But Jesus
said, "Touch my hands and my feet
so that you will know it is really me."

The disciples cheered! They were
very, very happy to see Jesus again.

Goodnight Prayer

Dear Jesus, even death couldn't stop you from coming back. With you, anything is possible!

Say with your mouth, "Jesus is Lord."
Believe in your heart that God raised him
from the dead. Then you will be saved.
—Romans 10:9

Jesus Goes to Heaven

Matthew 28:16–20, Luke 24:44–51; Acts 1:6–11

Jesus had told his disciples, "I gave my life so that you could be with me in heaven. I am going there to prepare a wonderful new home for you. When I come back the next time, I will take you with me."
But now it was time for Jesus to leave.

Jesus said, "God has given me
complete power over heaven and earth.
Go and tell everyone the good news.
Make new disciples. Baptize them and
teach them to obey my commandments.
Don't ever forget, I will always be
with you."

Then Jesus promised,
"I am coming back soon."

Goodnight Prayer

Jesus, I'm going to tell people all about
you, and the good things you've done.
I will be ready when you come back!

*[Jesus] said to them, "Go into all the world.
Preach the good news to everyone."*
—Mark 16:15